FOR ORGANS, PIANOS & ELECTRONIC KEYBOARDS

A

BEGINNI... FOR KEYBO...
UPDATED EDITION
WITH ONLINE AUDIO

C000163867

PLAYBACK+
Speed • Pitch • Balance • Loop

To access audio visit:
www.halleonard.com/mylibrary

Enter Code
4329-9404-8373-4863

Audio arrangements by Peter Deneff

ISBN 978-1-5400-6526-1

Visit Hal Leonard Online at
www.halleonard.com

Contact us:
Hal Leonard
7777 West Bluemound Road
Milwaukee, WI 53213
Email: info@halleonard.com

In Europe, contact:
Hal Leonard Europe Limited
42 Wigmore Street
Marylebone, London, W1U 2RN
Email: info@halleonardeurope.com

In Australia, contact:
Hal Leonard Australia Pty. Ltd.
4 Lentara Court
Cheltenham, Victoria, 3192 Australia
Email: info@halleonard.com.au

A BEGINNING SOUND

On most organs and electronic keyboards, there are controls that produce or enhance sounds. Some of these are **voice tabs** or **tonebars** – instrumental voices at different pitches. Some are **general controls**, such as Vibrato, Percussion, or Tremolo. A combination of voice tabs or tonebars and general controls is called **registration**.

Registration

A Registration Guide showing different combinations of voices and controls is available for most organ models. A general Registration Guide appears at the end of this book. A registration number appears above the music for each song.

- Match this number with the number on the Registration Guide.

- Set up the voice tabs or tonebars as indicated.

- And don't forget your imagination! Use it to experiment with various registrations of your choice.

BEGINNINGS VISUAL GUIDES

Keyboard guides are included for both upper and lower keyboards. These visual aids make it possible for you to easily learn the keys on your particular instrument. Remove and place the guides on the keyboards as shown in this illustration.

- If the letter names of the keys are already identified on your instrument, simply omit the upper keyboard guide.

- If you're playing left-hand accompaniment with a chord button or a one-key chord accompaniment feature, disregard the lower keyboard guide.

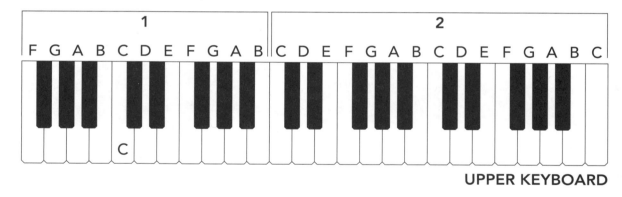

UPPER KEYBOARD

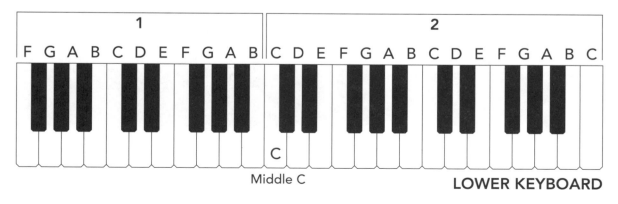

Middle C

LOWER KEYBOARD

Pedal labels are also included to help you become instantly familiar with the bass pedals. The following illustration shows the correct placement of these labels.

- If your instrument does not have pedals, or if you are using an automatic accompaniment feature that does not require the playing of pedals, disregard the pedal labels.

PEDALS

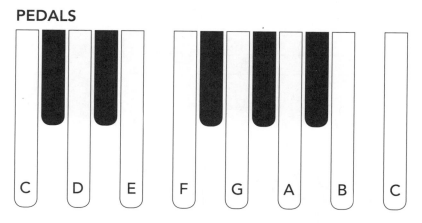

NOTATION

All songs are written in the exclusive E-Z PLAY® TODAY notation.

- A **staff** is five lines with spaces between them. Each line or space represents a lettered note.

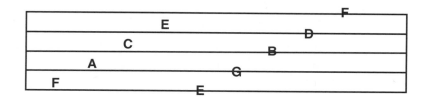

- Sometimes **ledger lines** are added above or below the staff to accommodate additional notes.

Ledger Lines

Ledger Lines

- The lettered notes correspond to lettered keys on the keyboard guide. As notes move down the staff, the corresponding keys move down (to the left) on the keyboard. As the notes move up the staff, they move up (to the right) on the keyboard.

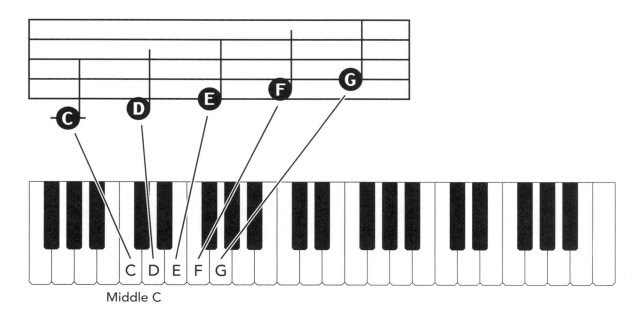

Middle C

Note Values

Each type of note has a specific **time value** that is measured in rhythmic beats.

QUARTER NOTE
1 Beat

HALF NOTE
2 Beats

DOTTED HALF NOTE
3 Beats

WHOLE NOTE
4 Beats

Each staff is divided by bar lines into sections called **measures**. A **double bar** indicates the end of a song.

Measure   Measure

Bar Line   Bar Line   Double
                                                  Bar Line

A **time signature** appears at the beginning of each song after the treble clef sign.

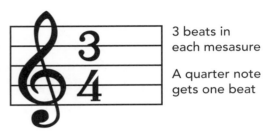

4 beats in each mesasure

A quarter note gets one beat

← Treble Clef

The **top number** indicates the number of rhythmic beats in each measure

The **bottom number** indicates the type of note that receives one beat. Thus, 4 indicates a quarter note.

3 beats in each mesasure

A quarter note gets one beat

Sometimes a note or notes appear at the beginning of a song that do not equal the number of beats indicated by the time signature. These are called **pickup notes**, and the missing beats are written at the end of the song.

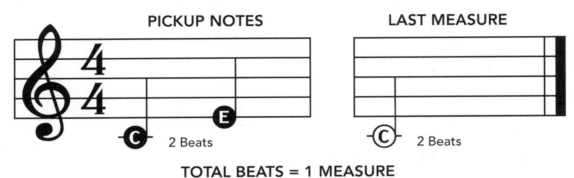

PICKUP NOTES

LAST MEASURE

2 Beats

2 Beats

TOTAL BEATS = 1 MEASURE

A **tie** is a curved line that connects notes of the same pitch (notes on the same line or space). Play the first note and then hold for the total time of all tied notes.

2 BEATS + 4 BEATS = 6 BEATS   4 BEATS + 4 BEATS = 8 BEATS

The Melody

Here's your first melody, "When the Saints Go Marching In." Before playing:

- Set at least one voice control for the upper keyboard.

- Place your entire right foot on the expression pedal, if your instrument has one. Press down with the ball of your foot to increase the volume; press back with your heel to decrease the volume.

- Now, carefully read the notes and play the corresponding keys with your right hand.

When the Saints Go Marching In

Music by James M. Black

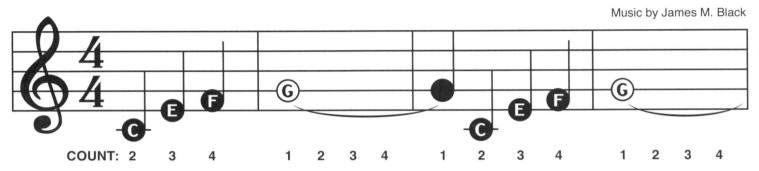

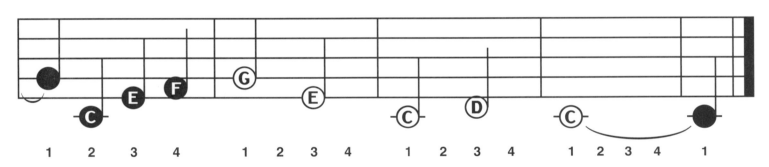

ACCOMPANIMENT

Accompaniment is the chord harmony played by your left hand. (Chords are combinations of three or more musical tones sounded simultaneously.)

In each arrangement, the accompaniment chords are indicated by boxed chord symbols that appear above the melody notes. These chord symbols indicate which chord to play. If N.C. (No Chord) appears above a section of a song, do not play a chord or pedal.

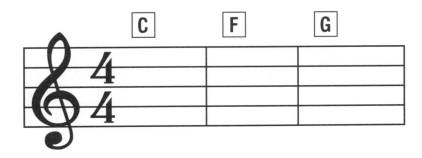

The number and type of chords on the many different automatic chord units vary. For this reason, alternate chord names are sometimes shown above the boxed symbols. If the boxed chord symbol does not appear on your instrument, play the alternate chord. Should both chords appear on your chord unit, play either chord.

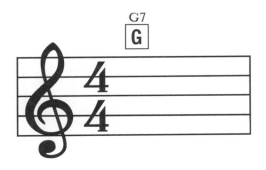

A CHORD SYSTEM FOR EVERYONE!

Chord accompaniment can be played in two ways. Read the following information carefully, then select the chord system you prefer.

1 One-Button (chord organ) or One-Key Chords

If you have a chord organ or a one-key chord unit on your instrument, press and hold the button or key indicated by the chord symbol. Each button or key produces a three- or four-note chord sound with a corresponding bass tone.

2 Standard Chord Positions

When playing standard chord positions, the positions (inversions) of the three- and four-note chords are strictly matters for your own choice. The suggested positions and fingerings for the C, G, and F chords are shown below. Bass pedals are often played with standard chord positions, although on some instruments the bass is produced automatically.

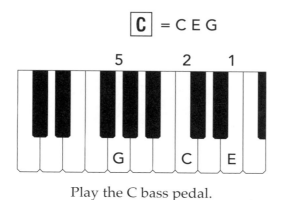

Play the C bass pedal.

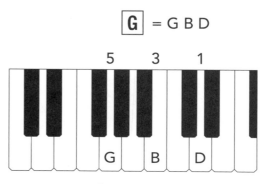

Play the G bass pedal.

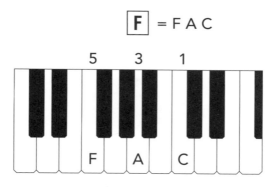

Play the F bass pedal.

For your reference, a **Chord Speller** of commonly used standard chord positions is located on page 46 of this book. Now play "When the Saints Go Marching In," using both right-hand melody and left-hand accompaniment.

When the Saints Go Marching In

Registration 2
Rhythm: Fox Trot or March

Words by Katherine E. Purvis
Music by James M. Black

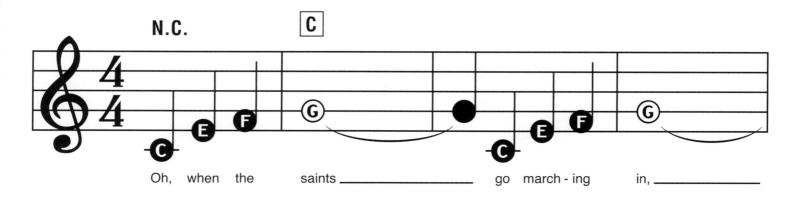

Oh, when the saints _____ go march-ing in,_____

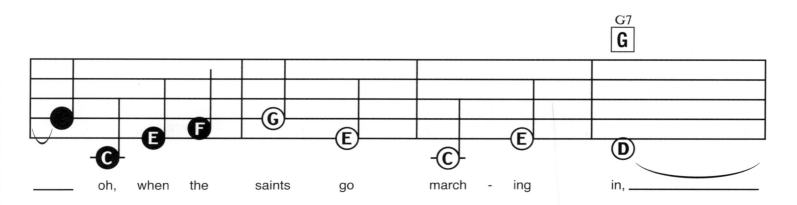

_____ oh, when the saints go march-ing in,_____

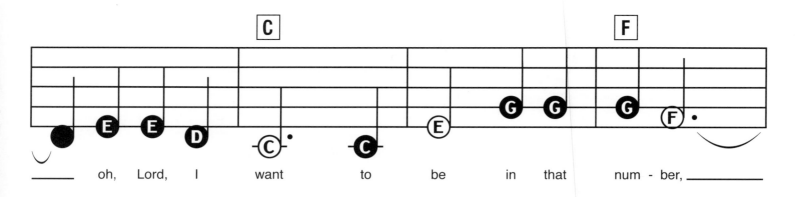

_____ oh, Lord, I want to be in that num-ber,_____

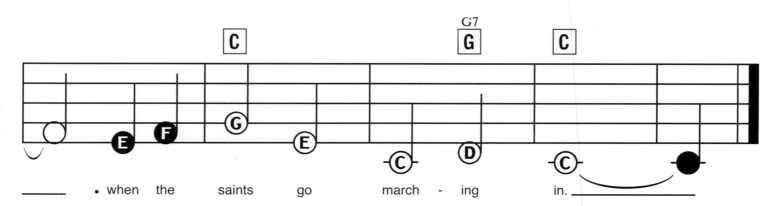

_____ when the saints go march-ing in._____

9

AUTOMATIC RHYTHM

The excitement created by an automatic rhythm will enhance your music, regardless of which left-hand chord system you select. Here are a few hints for the most effective use of your rhythm unit:

- Experiment with the various rhythms available on your unit. Select a rhythm pattern that complements each song. Sometimes it's fun to create an unusual or different mood by selecting a rhythm pattern not generally associated with the song. For example, you might try a rock rhythm with "When the Saints Go Marching In."

- Most rhythm units have a control that regulates the volume level of the percussion instruments. For Latin rhythms, the percussion instruments usually play a more prominent role than in a ballad-type rhythm, so adjust the volume control accordingly.

- Every rhythm has a tempo control that regulates the speed of the selected rhythm pattern. As you first begin to learn a song, adjust the tempo control to a slower speed until you can play the song with ease and accuracy.

- The tempo light flashes at predetermined time intervals. Watch the light for the speed of the rhythm and to determine when a rhythm pattern begins.

Play "When the Saints Go Marching In" again, this time adding an appropriate automatic rhythm, such as Fox Trot, Swing, Dixieland, or March.

INTRODUCING NEW NOTES

In the next two songs, there are three new notes: A, B, and another C.

- They appear like this on the staff.

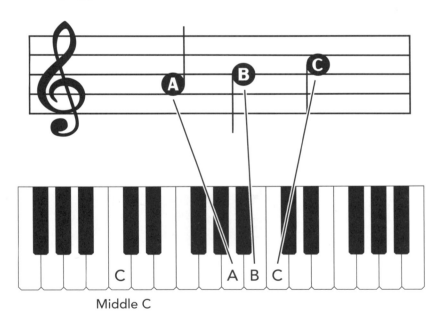

Middle C

- They correspond to these keys on the keyboard.

10

Kumbaya

Registration 3
Rhythm: Ballad or Latin

Congo Folksong

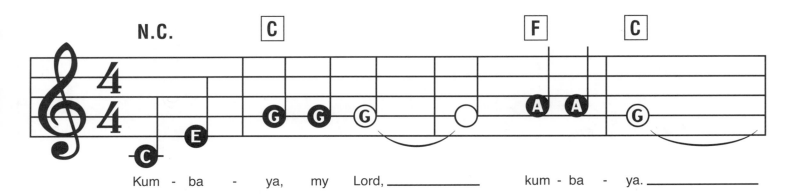

Kum - ba - ya, my Lord, _____ kum - ba - ya. _____

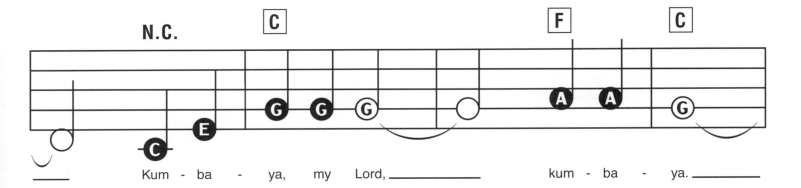

_____ Kum - ba - ya, my Lord, _____ kum - ba - ya. _____

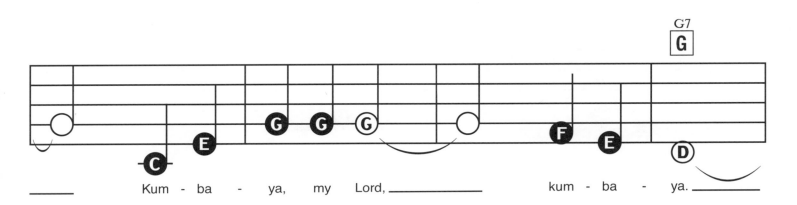

_____ Kum - ba - ya, my Lord, _____ kum - ba - ya.

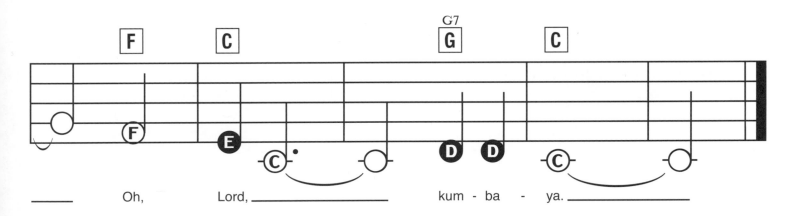

_____ Oh, Lord, _____ kum - ba - ya. _____

Marines' Hymn

Registration 2
Rhythm: March

Words by Henry C. Davis
Melody based on a theme by Jacques Offenbach

From the halls of Mon - te - zu -

ma to the shores of Trip - o - li, ____

we ____ fight our coun - try's bat -

tles in the air, on land, and sea. ____

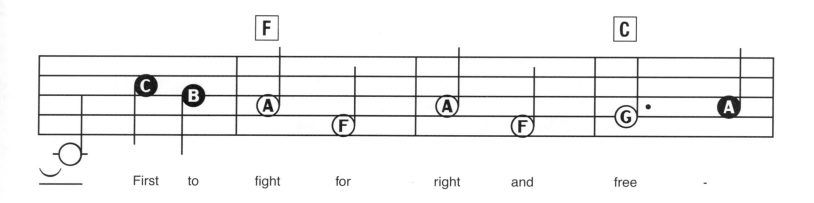

First to fight for right and free -

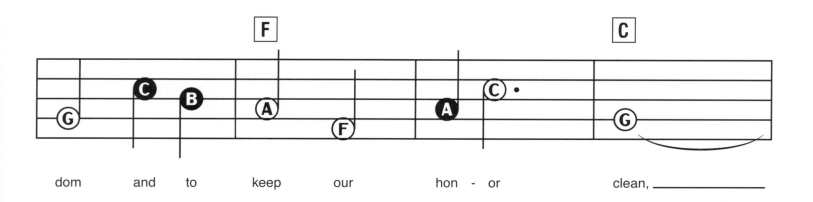

dom and to keep our hon - or clean, _____

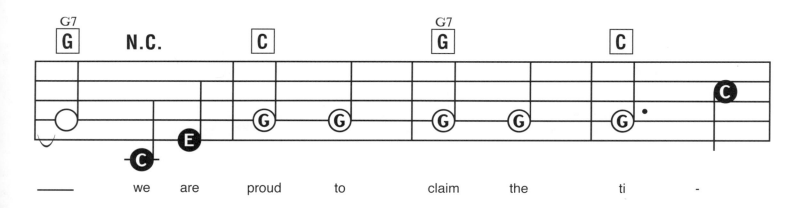

_____ we are proud to claim the ti -

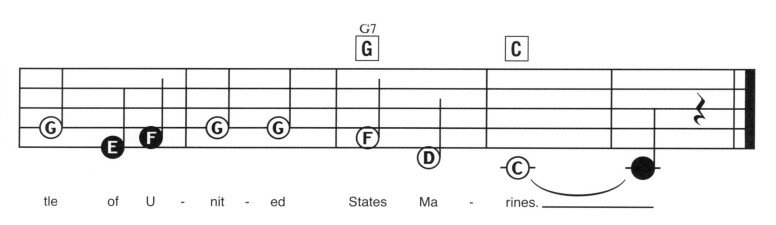

tle of U - nit - ed States Ma - rines. _____

INTRODUCING NEW NOTES

New D, E, and F notes are introduced in the next melodies.

- They appear like this on the staff.

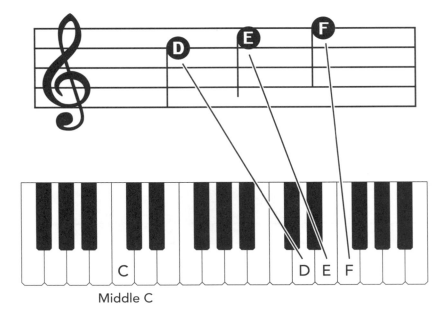

Middle C

- They correspond to these keys on the keyboard.

INTRODUCING RESTS

Rests indicate periods of silence. They correspond to the time values of notes having the same name.

QUARTER REST
1 Beat

HALF REST
2 Beats

WHOLE REST
Whole Measure

INTRODUCING REPEAT SIGNS

Repeat signs are used in a song when a section of the arrangement or the entire song is to be played again (repeated). Generally, repeat signs appear in sets of two.

- There will be one repeat sign (A) at the beginning of the section to be repeated.
- Play all the way to the repeat sign at the end of this section (B).
- Return to the first repeat sign (A) and play the section again.
- If there is no repeat sign (A), return to the beginning of the song.

INTRODUCING 1st AND 2nd ENDINGS

When two different endings appear within or at the end of a song, here's what to do:

- Play the song up through the first (1) ending.
- Repeat to the closest repeat sign, or back to the beginning.
- Play that section again, skip the first ending (1), but play the second ending (2).

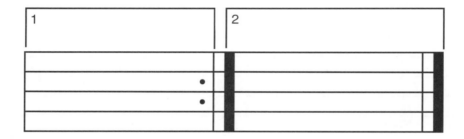

Old Folks at Home
(Swanee River)

Registration 9
Rhythm: Dixie or Shuffle

Words and Music by
Stephen C. Foster

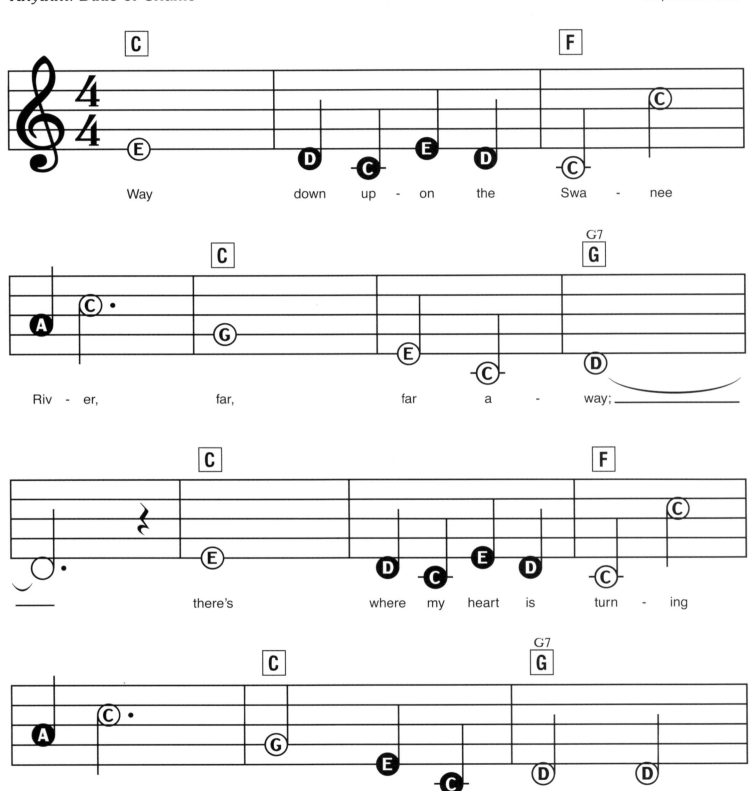

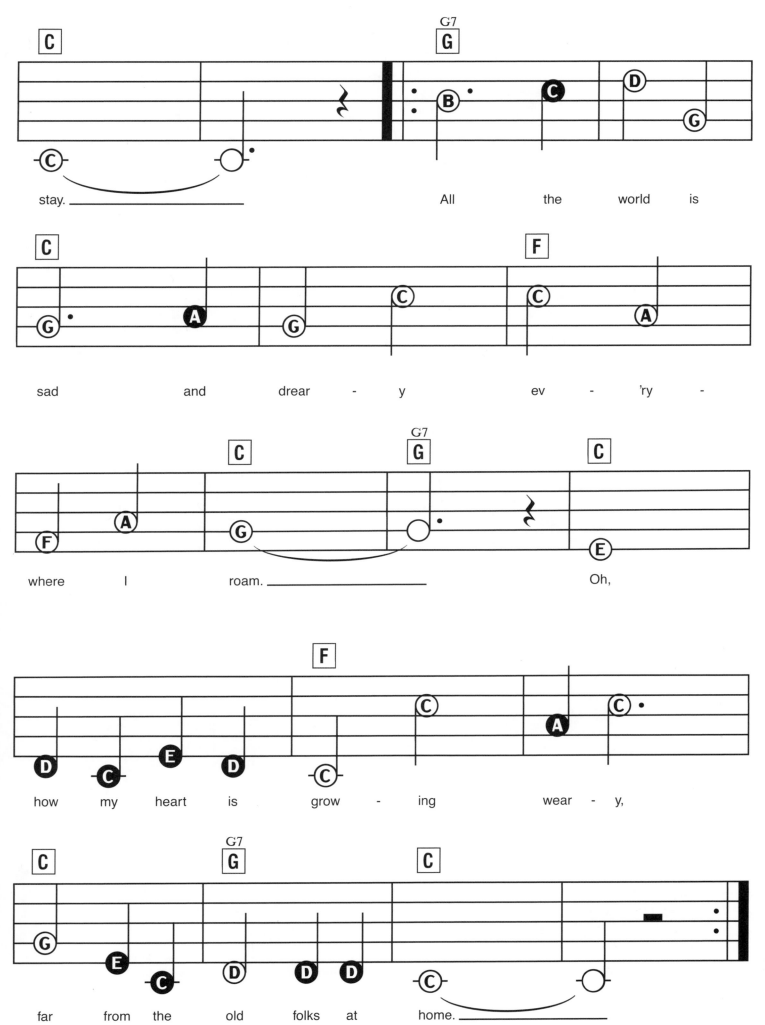

stay. _____ All the world is

sad and drear - y ev - 'ry -

where I roam. _____ Oh,

how my heart is grow - ing wear - y,

far from the old folks at home. _____

Yankee Doodle

Registration 2
Rhythm: March

Traditional

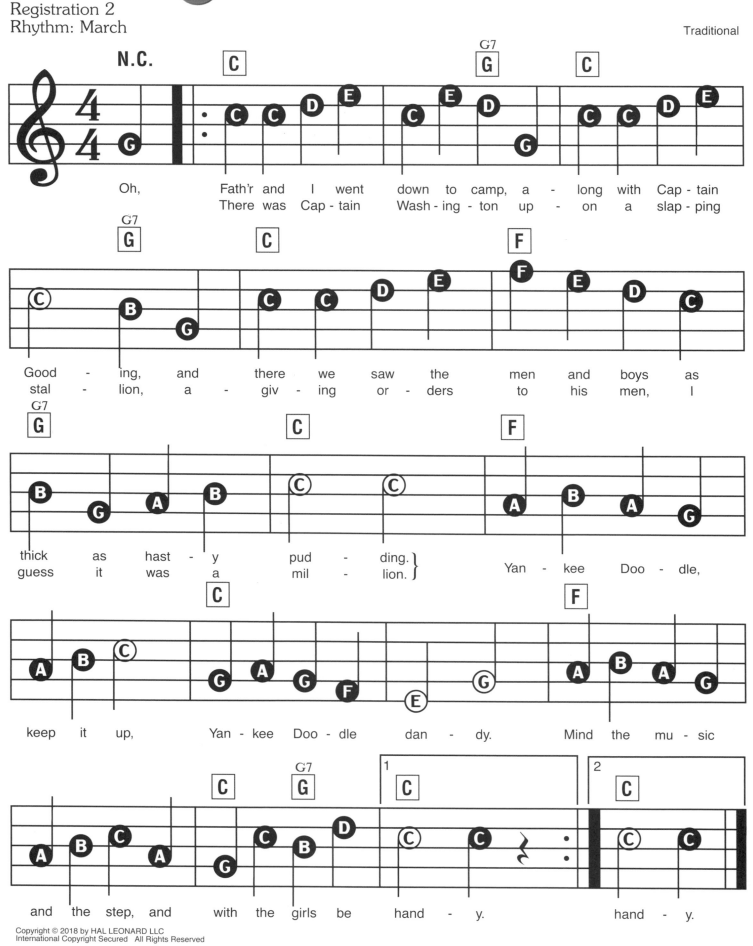

INTRODUCING HALF STEPS

A **half step** is the distance between any two adjacent keys on the keyboard. Half steps can be formed in three different ways.

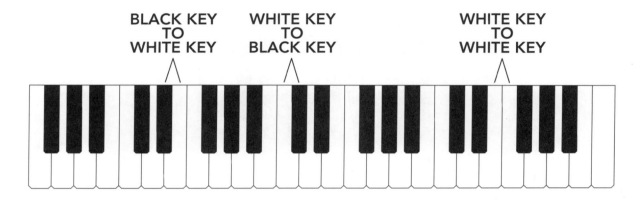

INTRODUCING THE FLAT SIGN (♭)

When a **flat sign** appears to the left of a note, lower the note one half step. In other words, play the first adjacent key to the left.

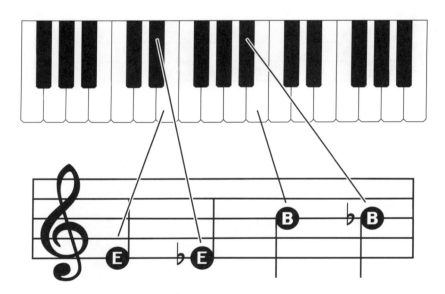

INTRODUCING A NEW CHORD: B♭

- **One key** or **chord button:** Locate the key or button labeled B♭.

- **Standard chord:** B♭ = B♭ D F

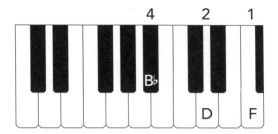

INTRODUCING THE FERMATA (𝄐)

When a **fermata** appears above or below a note, it means you should hold the note longer than its normal time value. Fermatas most often appear at the end of a song.

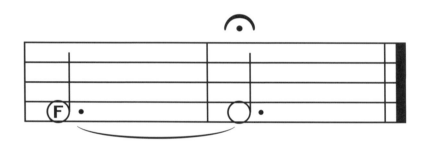

Aura Lee

Registration 4
Rhythm: Ballad or Fox Trot

Words by W.W. Fosdick
Music by George R. Poulton

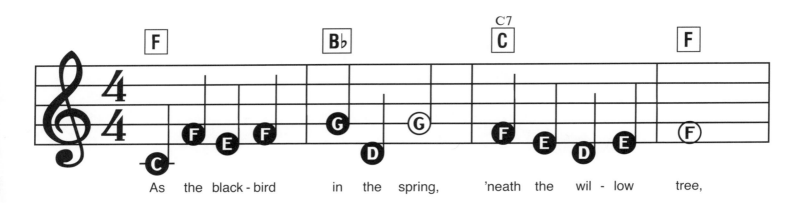

As the black-bird in the spring, 'neath the wil-low tree,

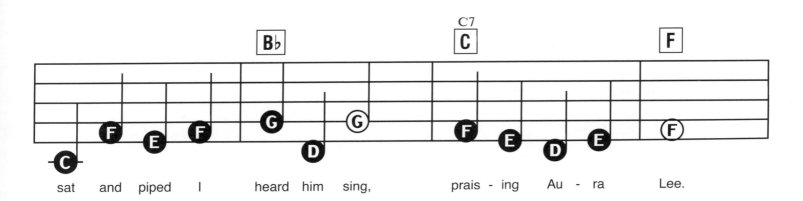

sat and piped I heard him sing, prais-ing Au-ra Lee.

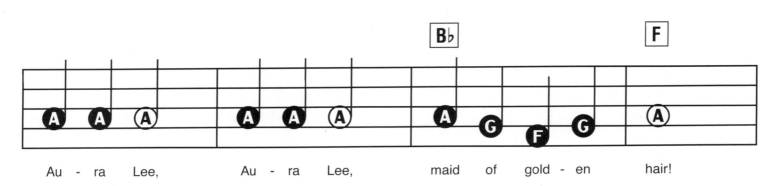

Au-ra Lee, Au-ra Lee, maid of gold-en hair!

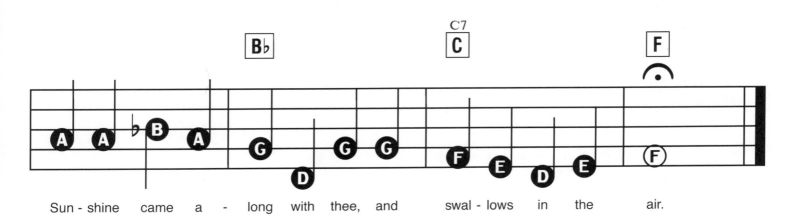

Sun-shine came a-long with thee, and swal-lows in the air.

INTRODUCING A NEW CHORD: Dm

One key or **chord button:** Locate the key(s) or button labeled Dm.

Standard chord: **Dm** = A D F

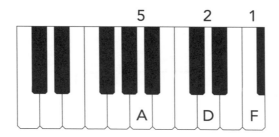

On Top of Old Smoky

Registration 4
Rhythm: Waltz

Kentucky Mountain Folksong

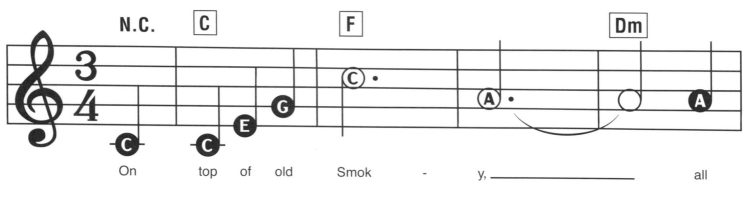

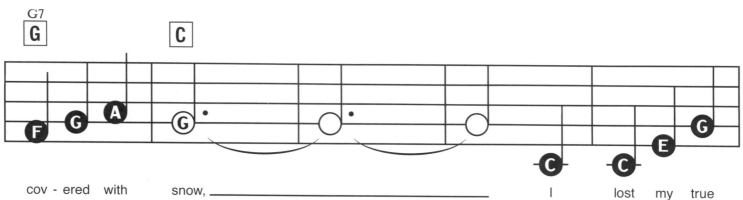

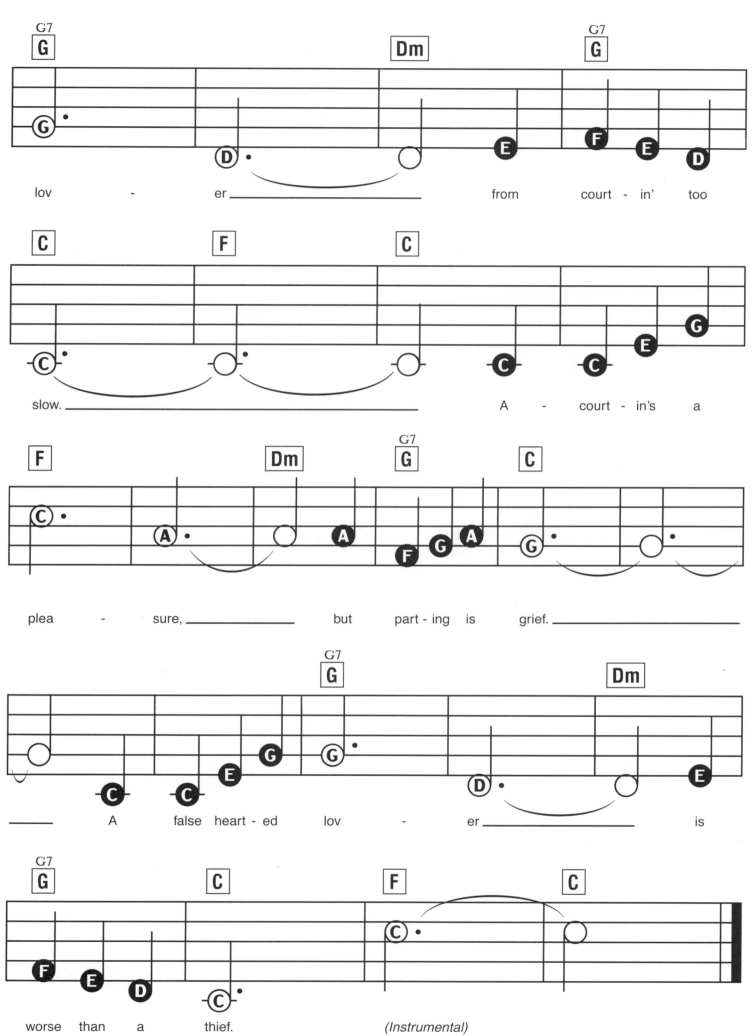

lov - er _____ from court - in' too slow. _____ A - court - in's a plea - sure, _____ but part - ing is grief. _____ A false heart - ed lov - er _____ is worse than a thief. *(Instrumental)*

INTRODUCING EIGHTH NOTES

- A single **eighth note** has a flag on its stem. It receives one half-beat.

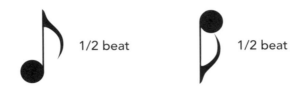

1/2 beat   1/2 beat

- Two or more eighth notes are written in a group and connected by a beam.

Two eighth notes equal one full beat   2 Beats

- To play and correctly count eighth notes, divide your counting of each beat into two parts by saying "and" between the numbered beats

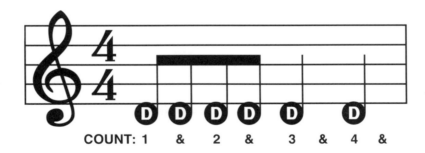

COUNT: 1   &   2   &   3   &   4   &

Skip to My Lou

Registration 4
Rhythm: Fox Trot or Swing

Traditional

F
A A F F A A A C
Choose your part - ners, skip to my Lou;

C7 / C
G G E E
choose your part - ners,

F
G G G B A A F F A A A C
skip to my Lou; choose your part - ners, skip to my Lou;

C7 / C
G A B A G F F
skip to my Lou, my dar - ling.

F
A A A F F F
Fly's in the but - ter - milk,

A A C G G G E E E G G B
shoo, fly, shoo; fly's in the but - ter - milk, shoo, fly, shoo;

F
A A A F F F A A C
fly's in the but - ter - milk, shoo, fly, shoo!

C7 / C
G A B A G
Skip to my Lou, my

F
F F
dar - ling.

INTRODUCING THE DOTTED-QUARTER NOTE

- A dot placed after any note increases the length of that note by one-half.

- As previously illustrated, the dotted-half note receives three beats.

HALF NOTE
2 Beats

\+

HALF of 2 (1)
1 Beat

=

DOTTED-HALF NOTE
3 Beats

- The same principle applies to the dotted-quarter note.

QUARTER NOTE
1 Beat

\+

HALF of 1 (1/2)
1/2 Beat

=

DOTTED-QUARTER NOTE
1 1/2 Beats

- The dotted-quarter note is usually followed by an eighth note.

1 1/2 Beats   1/2 Beat

- Study and play this counting example.

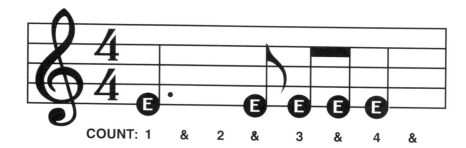

COUNT: 1   &   2   &   3   &   4   &

26

INTRODUCING THE SHARP SIGN (♯)

When a **sharp sign** appears to the left of any note, raise the note one half-step. In other words, play the first adjacent key to the right.

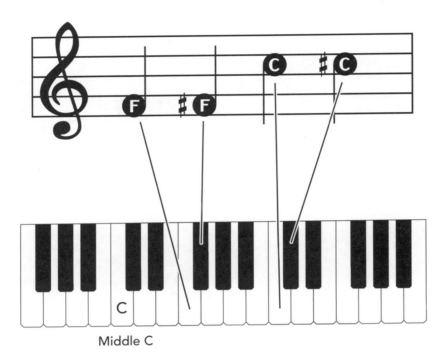

Middle C

INTRODUCING A NEW CHORD: D

- **One key** or **chord button:** Locate the key or button labeled D. If your automatic chord unit does not have the D chord, play the alternate chord D7.

- **Standard chord:** D = F♯ A D

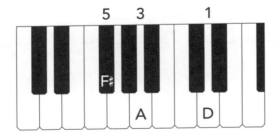

The Blue Tail Fly
(Jimmy Crack Corn)

Registration 4
Rhythm: Fox Trot

Words and Music by
Daniel Decatur Emmett

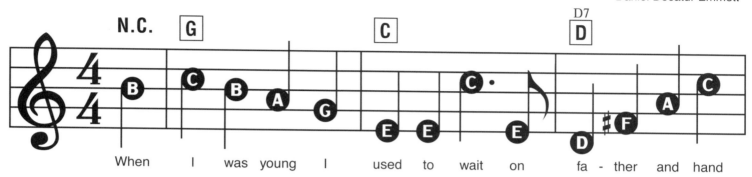

When I was young I used to wait on fa - ther and hand

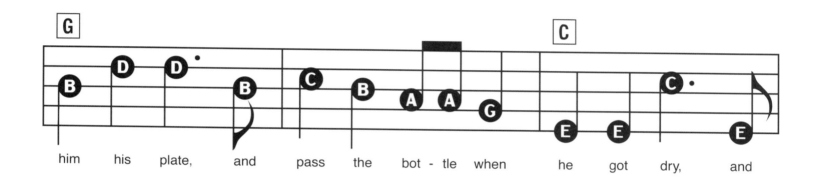

him his plate, and pass the bot - tle when he got dry, and

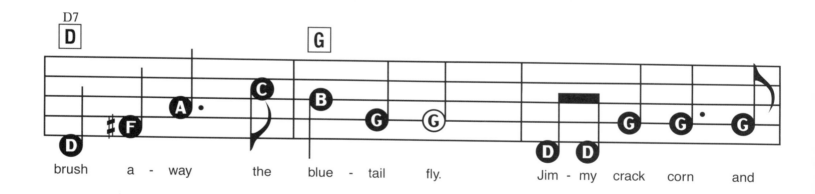

brush a - way the blue - tail fly. Jim - my crack corn and

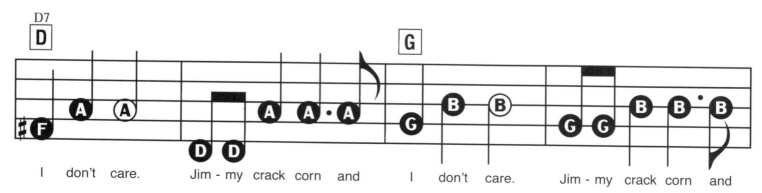

I don't care. Jim - my crack corn and I don't care. Jim - my crack corn and

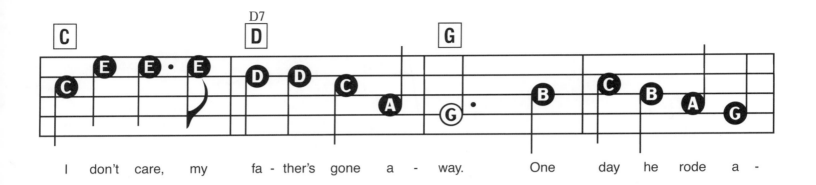

I don't care, my fa - ther's gone a - way. One day he rode a -

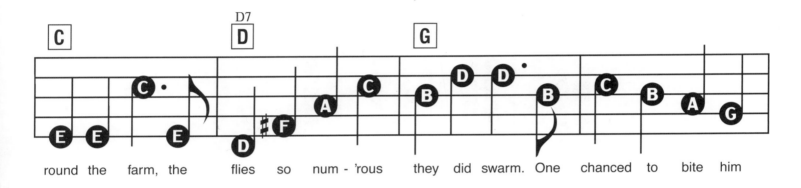

round the farm, the flies so num - 'rous they did swarm. One chanced to bite him

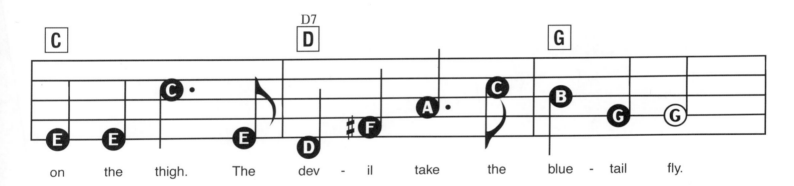

on the thigh. The dev - il take the blue - tail fly.

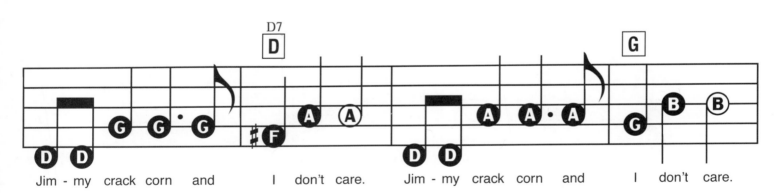

Jim - my crack corn and I don't care. Jim - my crack corn and I don't care.

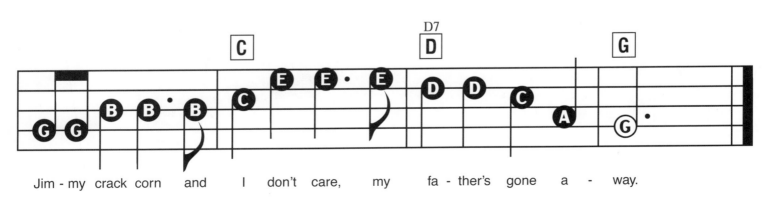

Jim - my crack corn and I don't care, my fa - ther's gone a - way.

INTRODUCING A NEW NOTE

To be able to play the next song, the well-known "lullaby" by Brahms, you'll need to learn the staff and keyboard location of another G.

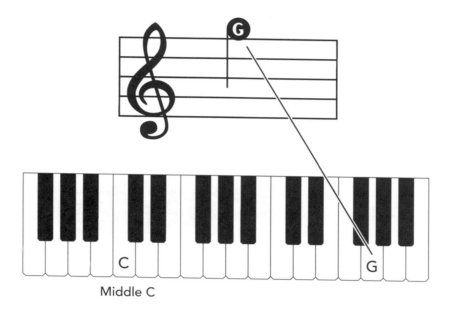

Middle C

INTRODUCING D.S. al CODA

D.S. al Coda is another type of repeat sign. The letters D.S. stand for dal segno. That's Italian for "from the sign." The entire term means to:

- Return to the sign 𝄋

- Repeat to this sign ⊕

- Skip to the section marked CODA and play to the end.

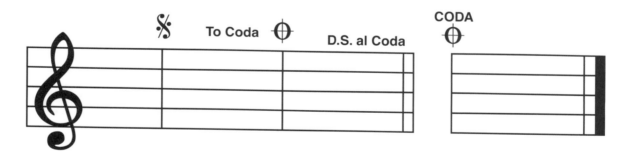

Apply this information as you learn "Down By the Riverside" on pages 32-33.

Lullaby
(Cradle Song)

Registration 1
Rhythm: Waltz

By Johannes Brahms

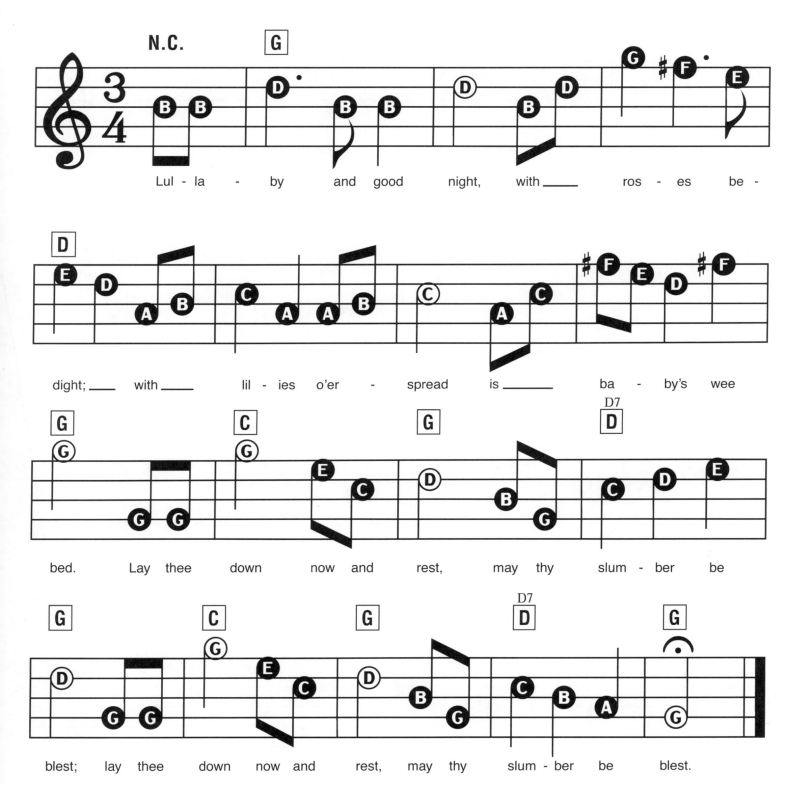

Down By the Riverside

Registration 7
Rhythm: Jazz or Swing

African-American Spiritual

N.C. % C

Gon - na   lay down   my   heav - y   load
put   on   my   long white robe   down by   the

G7
G   C

riv - er - side,   down by the   riv - er - side,   down by the

riv - er - side. {Gon - na   lay down   my   heav - y   load
                   Gon - na   put   on   my   long white robe}   down by the

Dm   G7
                            G   To Coda ⊕   C

riv - er - side and   stud - y _____   war   no   more. _____

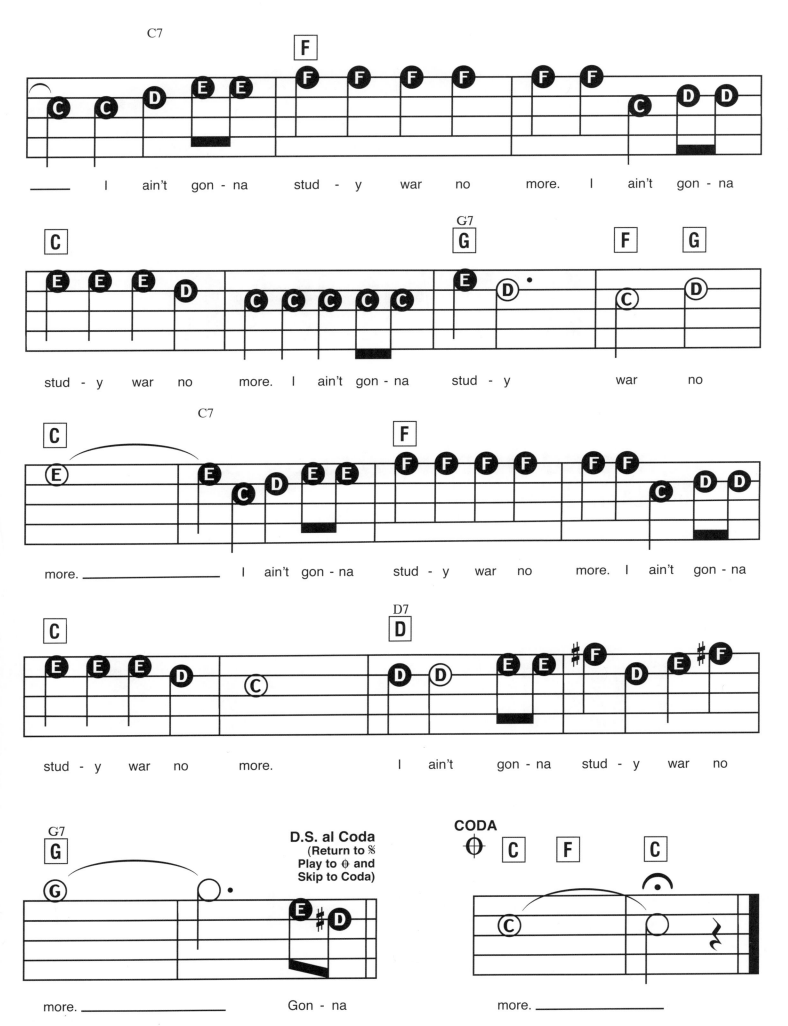

33

INTRODUCING A NEW NOTE

Learn the staff and keyboard location of this new A note before playing "Simple Gifts."

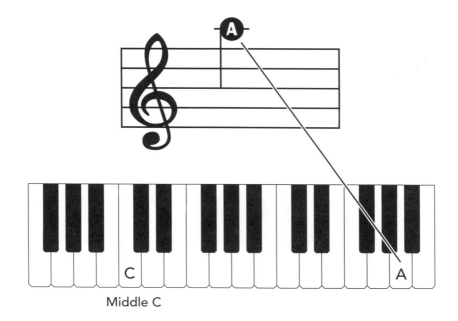

Middle C

INTRODUCING THREE NEW CHORDS:
Gm , Am , and A

Three new chords are used in the songs that follow.

One key or **chord button**: Locate the keys or buttons labeled Gm, Am, and A.

Standard chord:

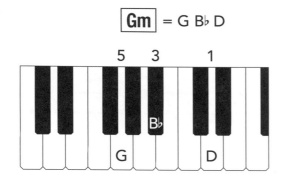

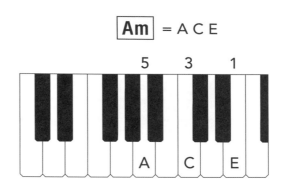

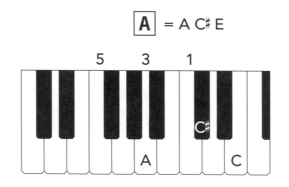

Simple Gifts

Registration 4
Rhythm: Folk

Traditional Shaker Hymn

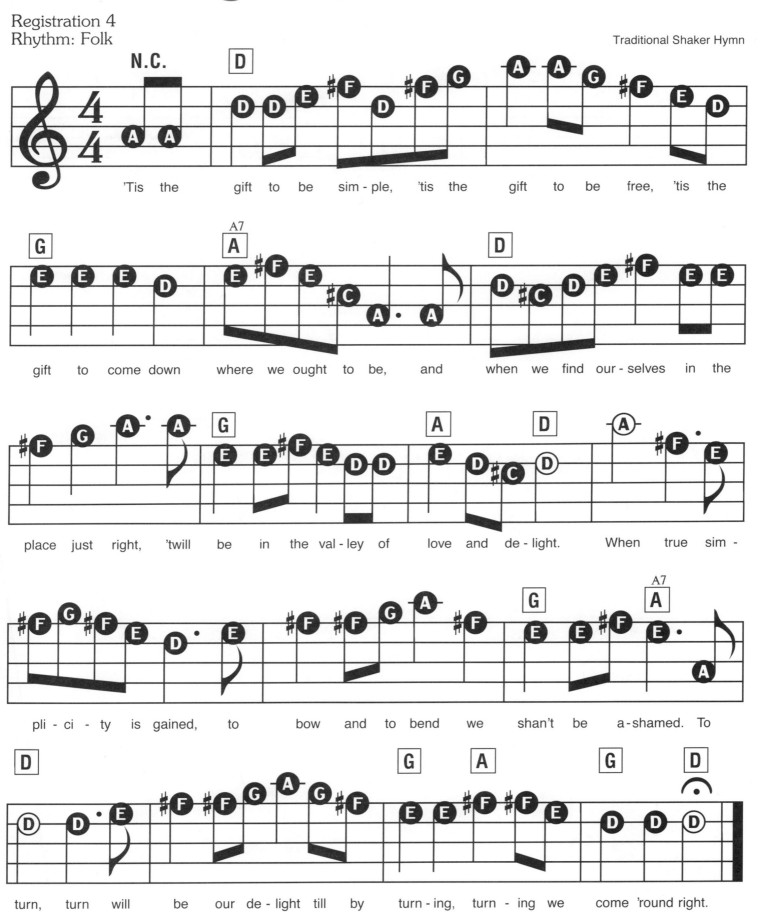

Danny Boy

Registration 8
Rhythm: Ballad

Words by Frederick Edward Weatherly
Traditional Irish Folk Melody

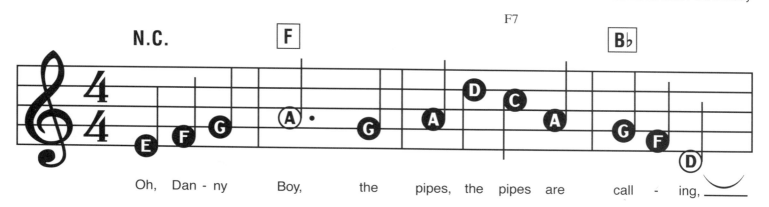

Oh, Dan - ny Boy, the pipes, the pipes are call - ing, _____

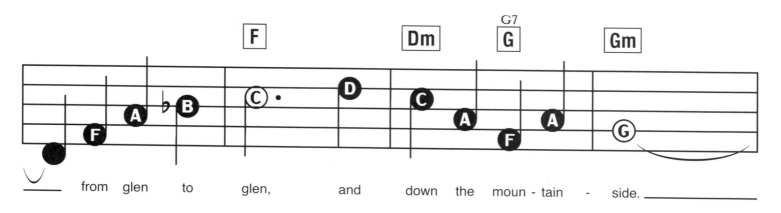

_____ from glen to glen, and down the moun - tain - side. _____

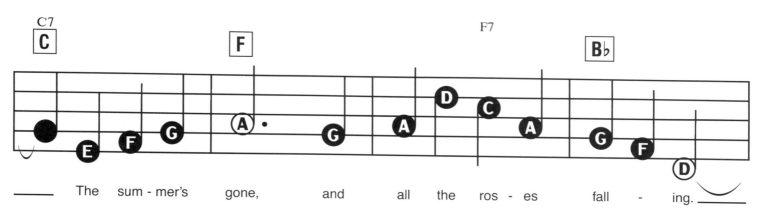

_____ The sum - mer's gone, and all the ros - es fall - ing. _____

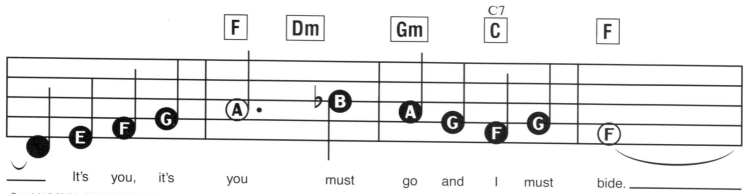

_____ It's you, it's you must go and I must bide. _____

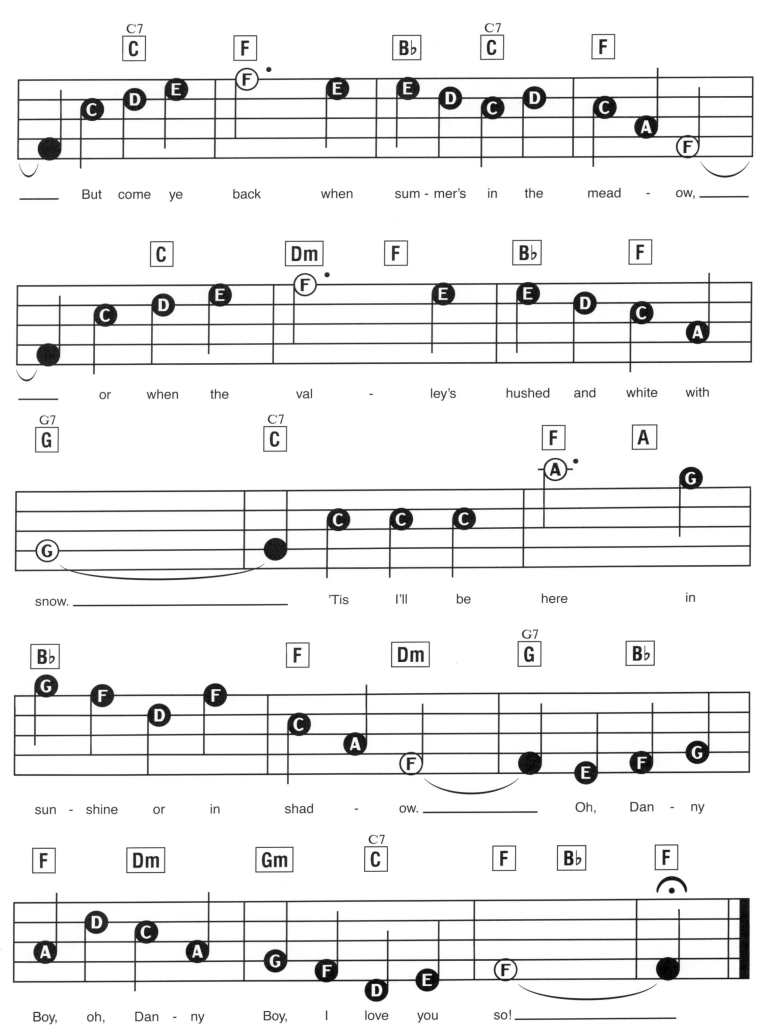

But come ye back when sum-mer's in the mead - ow, _____ or when the val - ley's hushed and white with snow. _____ 'Tis I'll be here in sun - shine or in shad - ow. _____ Oh, Dan - ny Boy, oh, Dan - ny Boy, I love you so! _____

Steal Away
(Steal Away to Jesus)

Registration 6
Rhythm: Ballad

Traditional Spiritual

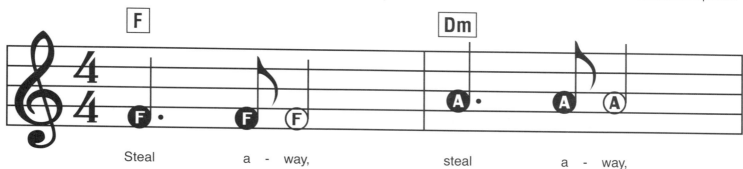

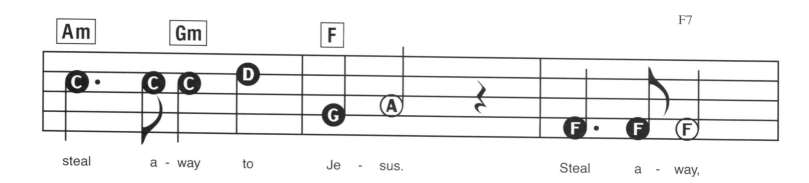

Steal a - way, steal a - way, steal a - way to Je - sus.

Steal a - way,

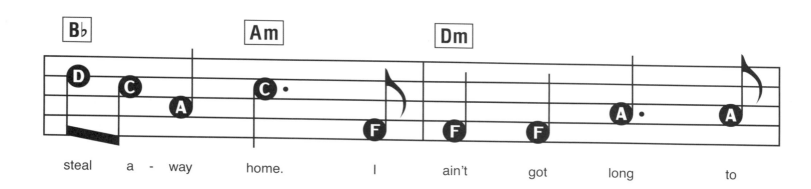

steal a - way home. I ain't got long to

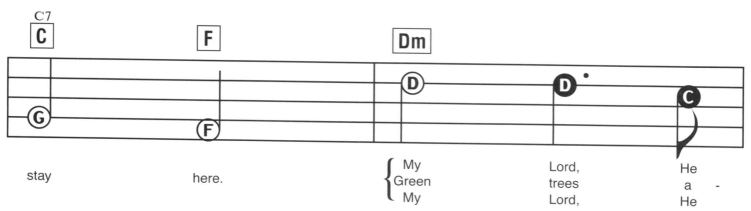

stay here.

My Lord, He
Green trees a -
My Lord, He

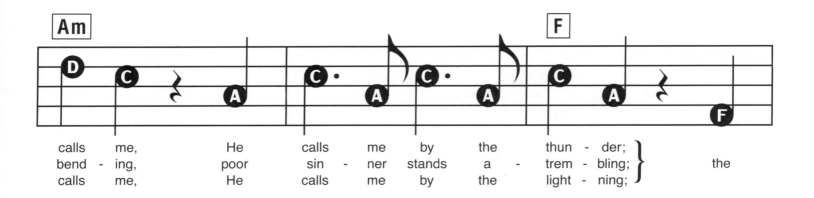

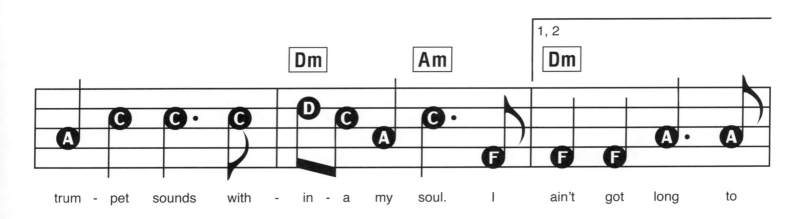

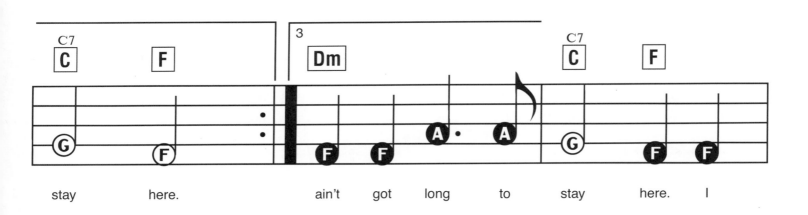

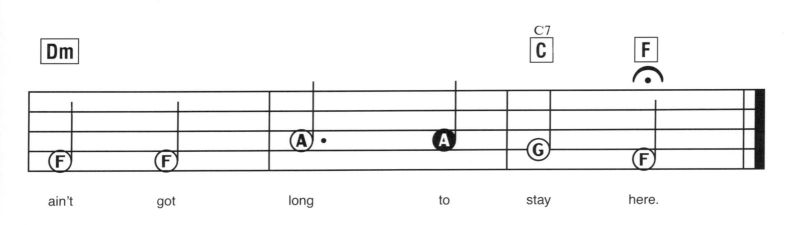

INTRODUCING THE EIGHTH REST

The **eighth rest** receives the same value as the eighth note, one half-beat:

INTRODUCING SYNCOPATION

Syncopation is the musical technique of playing certain melody notes on the "weak" beats of the measure. The "strong" beats of a measure are the numbered beats. The "weak" beats are the "and" beats.

NON-SYNCOPATED

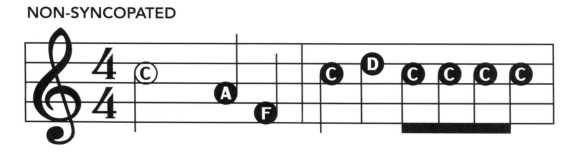

SYNCOPATED

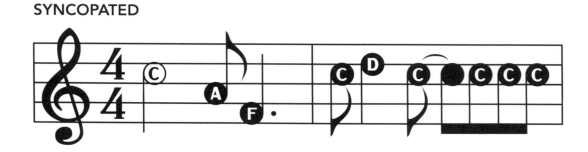

INTRODUCING REPEAT AND FADE

The term **Repeat and Fade** appears at the end of "He's Got the Whole World in His Hands." Return to the repeat sign near the beginning of the song. Play again and gradually reduce the volume level, creating a fade effect.

Somebody's Knocking at Your Door

Registration 8
Rhythm: Fox Trot or None

African-American Spiritual

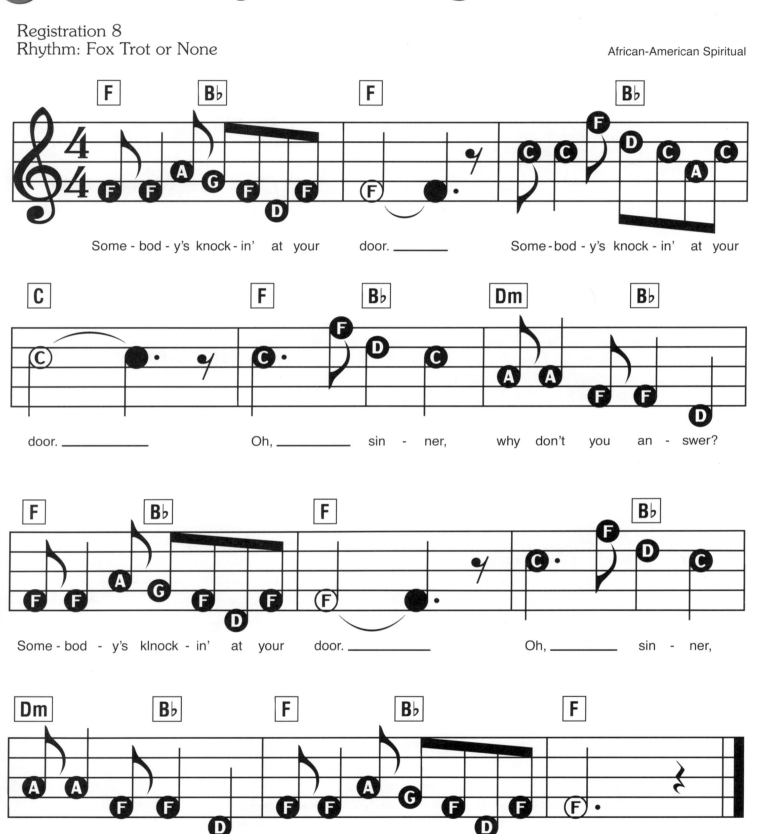

He's Got the Whole World in His Hands

Registration 1
Rhythm: Swing

Traditional Spiritual

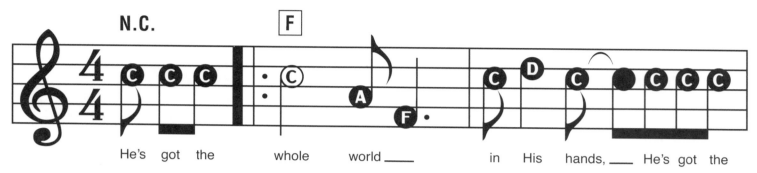

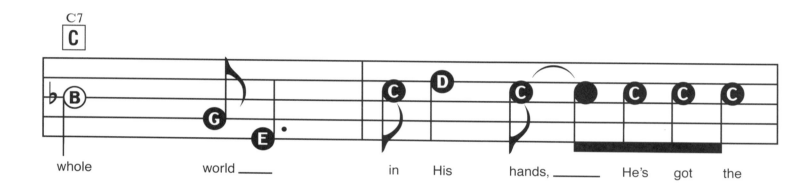

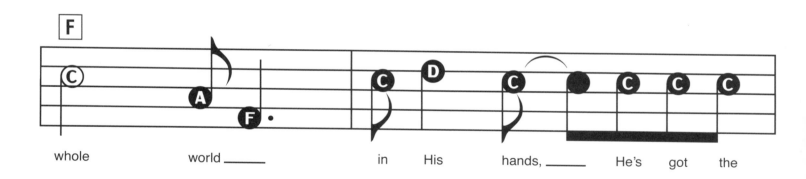

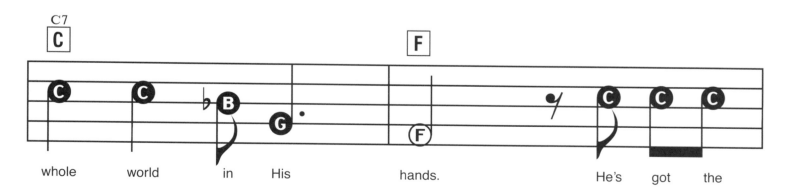

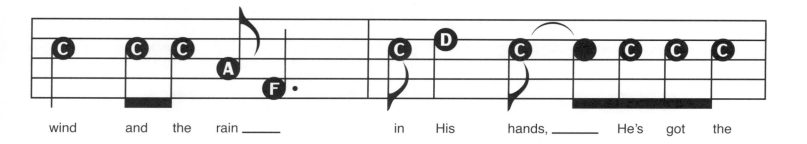

wind   and   the   rain _____   in   His   hands, _____   He's   got   the

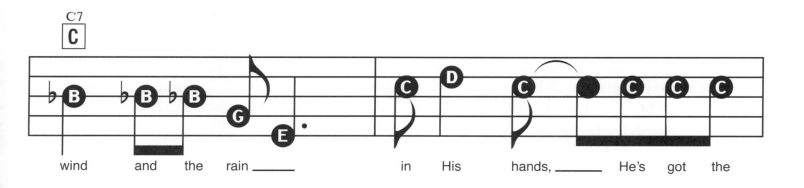

wind   and   the   rain _____   in   His   hands, _____   He's   got   the

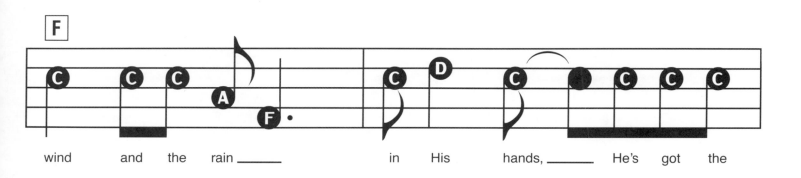

wind   and   the   rain _____   in   His   hands, _____   He's   got   the

Repeat and Fade

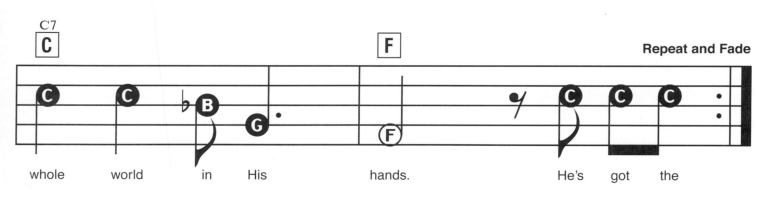

whole   world   in   His   hands.   He's   got   the

MUSIC NOTATION AND TERMS

For your reference, the following is a review of music notation and terms introduced in *Beginnings for Keyboards, Book A*.

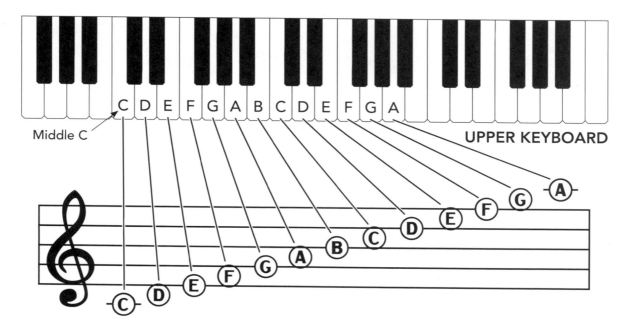

NOTE VALUES

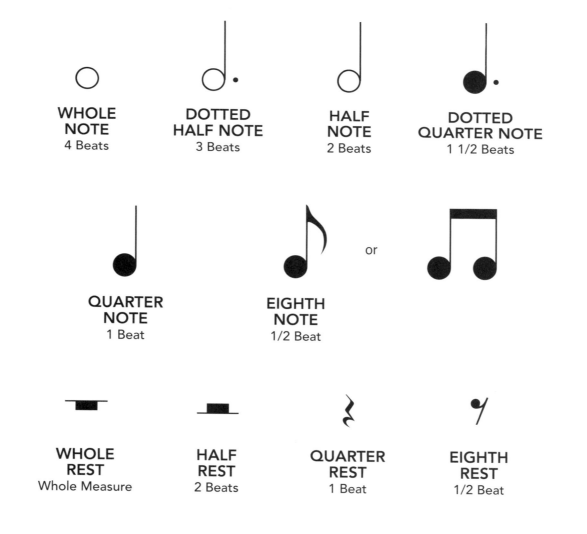

WHOLE NOTE	DOTTED HALF NOTE	HALF NOTE	DOTTED QUARTER NOTE
4 Beats	3 Beats	2 Beats	1 1/2 Beats

QUARTER NOTE
1 Beat

EIGHTH NOTE
1/2 Beat

or

WHOLE REST
Whole Measure

HALF REST
2 Beats

QUARTER REST
1 Beat

EIGHTH REST
1/2 Beat

REPEAT SIGNS

D.S. al Coda: Return to 𝄋, play until "To Coda," skip to CODA section.

Repeat and Fade: Repeat to beginning or to last repeat sign, then gradually fade out by decreasing the volume.

CHORDS

One Key or **Chord Button**

Standard Chord Positions: Refer to the Chord Speller Chart on page 46 for playing chords used in the E-Z PLAY® TODAY music arrangements.

N.C.

N.C. is an abbreviation for No Chord. Do not play a chord or pedal until the next chord symbol appears.

CHORD SPELLER CHART
of Standard Chord Positions

For those who play standard chord positions, all chords found in the E-Z PLAY® TODAY music arrangements are shown here in the most commonly used chord positions. Suggested fingering is also indicated, but feel free to use alternate fingerings.

CHORD FAMILY Abbrev.	MAJOR	MINOR (m)	7TH (7)
C	5 2 1 G – C – E	5 2 1 G – C – E♭	5 3 2 1 G – B♭ – C – E
D♭	5 2 1 A♭ – D♭ – F	5 2 1 A♭ – D♭ – E	5 3 2 1 A♭ – B – D♭ – F
D	5 3 1 F# – A – D	5 2 1 A – D – F	5 3 2 1 F# – A – C – D
E♭	5 3 1 G – B♭ – E♭	5 3 1 G♭ – B♭ – E♭	5 3 2 1 G – B♭ – D♭ – E♭
E	5 3 1 G# – B – E	5 3 1 G – B – E	5 3 2 1 G# – B – D – E
F	4 2 1 A – C – F	4 2 1 A♭ – C – F	5 3 2 1 A – C – E♭ – F
F#	4 2 1 F# – A# – C#	4 2 1 F# – A – C#	5 3 2 1 F# – A# – C# – E
G	5 3 1 G – B – D	5 3 1 G – B♭ – D	5 3 2 1 G – B – D – F
A♭	4 2 1 A♭ – C – E♭	4 2 1 A♭ – B – E♭	5 3 2 1 A♭ – C – E♭ – G♭
A	4 2 1 A – C# – E	4 2 1 A – C – E	5 4 2 1 G – A – C# – E
B♭	4 2 1 B♭ – D – F	4 2 1 B♭ – D♭ – F	5 4 2 1 A♭ – B♭ – D – F
B	5 2 1 F# – B – D#	5 2 1 F# – B – D	5 3 2 1 F# – A – B – D#

Registration Guide

- Match the Registration number on the song to the corresponding numbered category below. Select and activate an instrumental sound available on your instrument.

- Choose an automatic rhythm appropriate to the mood and style of the song. (Consult your Owner's Guide for proper operation of automatic rhythm features.)

- Adjust the tempo and volume controls to comfortable settings.

Registration

1	Mellow	Flutes, Clarinet, Oboe, Flugel Horn, Trombone, French Horn, Organ Flutes
2	Ensemble	Brass Section, Sax Section, Wind Ensemble, Full Organ, Theater Organ
3	Strings	Violin, Viola, Cello, Fiddle, String Ensemble, Pizzicato, Organ Strings
4	Guitars	Acoustic/Electric Guitars, Banjo, Mandolin, Dulcimer, Ukulele, Hawaiian Guitar
5	Mallets	Vibraphone, Marimba, Xylophone, Steel Drums, Bells, Celesta, Chimes
6	Liturgical	Pipe Organ, Hand Bells, Vocal Ensemble, Choir, Organ Flutes
7	Bright	Saxophones, Trumpet, Mute Trumpet, Synth Leads, Jazz/Gospel Organs
8	Piano	Piano, Electric Piano, Honky Tonk Piano, Harpsichord, Clavi
9	Novelty	Melodic Percussion, Wah Trumpet, Synth, Whistle, Kazoo, Perc. Organ
10	Bellows	Accordion, French Accordion, Mussette, Harmonica, Pump Organ, Bagpipes

E-Z PLAY® TODAY PUBLICATIONS

The E-Z Play® Today songbook series is the shortest distance between beginning music and playing fun! Check out this list of highlights and visit www.halleonard.com for a complete listing of all volumes and songlists.

HAL•LEONARD

Prices, contents, and availability subject to change without notice.